Red Fox in Winter

D0290903

Something to Think About . . .

Did you know?

*The red fox is part of the dog family. Its Latin name is *Vulpes fulva*. A red fox can run up to 30 miles (48 kilometers) per hour.

*Foxes are known for their cleverness and for their playfulness.

*A male fox, called a dog, is slightly larger than a female, which is called a vixen.

*Red foxes are found in most places in the world.

*A red fox weighs about 15 pounds (7 kilograms). It is about 36 inches (90 centimeters) long. Red foxes may live for up to 14 years.

Red Fox in Winter

by Janet Craig

illustrated by Janice Kinnealy

SCHOLASTIC INC.

New York Toronto London Auckland Sydney
Mexico City New Delhi Hong Kong Buenos Aires

No part of this publication may be reproduced in whole or in part,
or stored in a retrieval system, or transmitted in any form or by any means,
electronic, mechanical, photocopying, recording, or otherwise, without written
permission of the publisher. For information regarding permission, write to
Scholastic Inc., Attention: Permissions Department, 557 Broadway, New York, NY 10012.

ISBN 0-439-65214-6

Copyright © 1997 by Troll Communications L.L.C. All rights reserved.
Published by Scholastic Inc. SCHOLASTIC and associated logos are trademarks
and/or registered trademarks of Scholastic Inc.

12 11 10 9 8 7 6 5 4 3   5 6 7 8 9/0

Printed in the U.S.A.   08

First Scholastic printing, January 2004

Brrr! It's cold!
But someone is warm.

Who is it?
Its ears are pointed.
Its nose is pointed, too.

Its fur is red.
Its bushy tail has a white tip.

Who is it?
It's a red fox!

When night comes, the fox's
eyes open wide.
Like a cat, the fox sees well at night.
She sniffs the air.
She smells a mouse.

It is time to hunt for food.
The fox and her mate run quickly.
They hunt near the edge of the woods.

Foxes have very good hearing.
They can hear a mouse that is 100 feet
(30 meters) away.

The fox jumps
high.

It pounces on
the mouse.

Foxes also like to eat rabbits, birds, insects, and berries.

Sometimes the fox buries extra food,
just like a dog.
Later it comes back to have a snack.

Even in cold weather, red foxes sleep
in the open.
But now the female fox is about to
have pups.

The fox and her mate look for a home. They find an old groundhog or badger hole.

They dig more tunnels and doors.
Now their home is ready.
It is called a den.

Look at the pups.
How small they are!
Their eyes will not
open for nine days.

The mother and father take care of
their pups.
The pups drink milk from their mother.

When an enemy comes, the father
tries to trick it.
He lets the enemy chase him.
Then he leads the animal
far from the den.

Now the pups are five weeks old.

Their parents bring them live mice to eat.
The pups play.
They jump and pounce.

Then the parents
show the young
foxes how to hunt.

By late summer, the foxes are ready to leave the den.

Each young fox sets out on its
own.
The mother and father each set out
alone, too. They will meet again
next winter.
Then it will be time to start a new family.

Brrr! It's cold!
But someone is warm.
It's the red fox in winter!

Index